SSI Monograph

CIVILIAN SKILLS FOR AFRICAN MILITARY OFFICERS TO RESOLVE THE INFRASTRUCTURE, ECONOMIC DEVELOPMENT, AND STABILITY CRISIS IN SUB-SAHARAN AFRICA

Diane E. Chido

March 2011

*****

Comments pertaining to this report are invited and should be forwarded to: Director, Strategic Studies Institute, U.S. Army War College, 122 Forbes Ave, Carlisle, PA 17013-5244.

*****

Special thanks are extended to my very able research assistant, Lieutenant Katherine Porter, who finished at the top of the U.S. 2010 ROTC class. Any errors or omissions are the sole responsibility of the author.

*****

All Strategic Studies Institute (SSI) publications may be downloaded free of charge from the SSI website. Hard copies of this report may also be obtained free of charge while supplies last by placing an order on the SSI website. The SSI website address is: *www.StrategicStudiesInstitute.army.mil*.

*****

The Strategic Studies Institute publishes a monthly e-mail newsletter to update the national security community on the research of our analysts, recent and forthcoming publications, and upcoming conferences sponsored by the Institute. Each newsletter also provides a strategic commentary by one of our research analysts. If you are interested in receiving this newsletter, please subscribe on the SSI website at *www.StrategicStudiesInstitute. army.mil/newsletter/*.

FOREWORD

In the United States, we often think of the military as an alternative to college, as a professional training ground, for a wide variety of skills that may include computer science, electronics, cooking, or medicine. We have comprehensive job placement and support programs for separating service members. Our military training includes discipline, teaming concepts, and a respect for civil society, traits expected to remain with a military member for life.

Through U.S. Africa Command (USAFRICOM) partnership programs in Sub-Saharan Africa, many officers are currently benefitting from military-to-military training opportunities to learn aspects of military science and other basic training. A small number of officers will gain valuable skills they can use throughout their military careers or even in civilian life.

Ms. Diane Chido argues that if our own military service members on separation or retirement faced return to their hometowns with uncertain pension payments and no transferable skills, along with a sudden loss of purpose and prestige, our country would not be as stable as it is. Remove our consistent training in discipline, respect for civilian authority, and loyalty to the national structure, and we have a greater chance of instability. If we add a complete lack of energy, telecommunications, and transportation infrastructure to support even basic economic development, we have a situation resembling that of many ethnically divided African countries, with no employment opportunities in the civilian sphere and where the rule of law exists only for some.

Retirement-age military officers have historically engaged in coups in numerous African countries, and frequently civil wars reignite, even with robust disarmament, demobilization, and reintegration (DDR) programs. If these experienced officers, accustomed to leading and doing, are given the skills to manage construction projects and the knowledge to design and build power stations, dams, bridges, and roads, and if noncommissioned officers are trained to run and maintain these projects once built; those who pledged to serve their country in uniform could continue to do so with pride and purpose while wearing mufti. Infrastructure development and enhanced economic opportunity would no longer be entirely reliant on expensive foreign aid and experts. Above all, the threat of destabilization would be reduced.

DOUGLAS C. LOVELACE, JR.
Director
Strategic Studies Institute

ABOUT THE AUTHOR

DIANE E. CHIDO is an adjunct professor of intelligence studies at the Mercyhurst College Institute for Intelligence Studies. She also serves as a faculty advisor for student researchers on numerous Department of Defense contracts with the Center for Intelligence Research, Analysis, and Training. She is the President of DC Analytics, a research and analysis firm formed in October 2008. She is currently subcontracted as a cultural awareness expert on the Horn of Africa, assisting in creating training materials for U.S. troops. She has over 15 years of experience in research with the International Monetary Fund and with the Brookings Institution Foreign Policy Program. Ms. Chido publishes widely on intelligence analysis, ethnic conflict, and international security topics. She completed the U.S. Army Culture Center's train-the-trainer course on Cultural Awareness in the Horn of Africa and holds a Graduate Certificate in Russian/East European Studies, a BA in international studies and Russian studies, an MA in Russian language, and an MS in applied intelligence analysis.

SUMMARY

United States Africa Command (USAFRICOM) has pledged to work toward stability in Africa through enhanced partnerships with African countries, mainly through military-to-military training. This is likely to be highly beneficial to serving officers in African military institutions. However, military training alone does not prepare those officers for separation from service and an uncertain future in societies that do not pay pensions on time, if at all, and that do not offer economic opportunities in general, but especially not to those without needed skills.

USAFRICOM is at a unique point in its engagement with the continent as it develops programs and adjusts its approach. This is the optimum time to create a holistic framework in which to focus on training and to give these officers sustainable skills in engineering and other technical fields as part of the military curriculum. Such skills are urgently needed to construct and maintain the national infrastructures now lacking in Africa. Such infrastructures are essential if Africa is to move into the new economy. Moreover, such an effort will ultimately provide opportunities for retired service members to continue to contribute to building the societies they once served to protect.

CIVILIAN SKILLS FOR AFRICAN MILITARY OFFICERS TO RESOLVE THE INFRASTRUCTURE, ECONOMIC DEVELOPMENT, AND STABILITY CRISIS IN SUB-SAHARAN AFRICA

PROBLEMS OF STABILITY IN SUB-SAHARAN AFRICA

> Quintius [Cincinnatus] laid down his dictatorship on the sixteenth day, having received it for six months.[1]
>
> Livy

Like Cincinnatus, who peacefully returned to his family farm at the end of his agreed term as Roman military dictator, retiring American military officers typically look forward to promising second careers. These may be in the private sector, either as contractors to the military or consultants in various capacities, or by entering a field in which they were trained while in the service, such as accounting, engineering, information management, or medicine.

If these individuals faced simply heading back to their hometowns with uncertain pension payments and no transferable skills, could we assume that such a dire decline in their fortunes, along with a sudden loss of prestige and purpose, would not adversely affect American social stability? It might not, because so much of our military training emphasizes discipline and loyalty to the nation. Would that be enough, though?

A common characteristic of Sub-Saharan Africa is lack of economic opportunity. This lack underpins its history of instability, which is particularly pervasive in post-conflict societies. Such societies tend repeatedly to descend into conflict when economic interests begin to collide. Lieutenant Colonel Clarence Bouchat's January 2010 Strategic Studies Institute (SSI) publication, *Security and Stability in Africa: A Development Approach*, provides "a primer for military and government staff members who may be unfamiliar with Africa but are assigned duties that involve participation in African affairs." Bouchat's paper "lays a foundation as to how and why the U.S. Government, and especially the military, might become involved in improving African economic development and political governance in order to attain security and stability."

Bouchat also explains that,

> Economic activities are the most central of all human endeavors. Although rich in human and geographic diversity, Africa has fallen behind the rest of the world in its economic development, adversely impacting African aspirations. . . . [E]conomic development and good governance need to be the basis of security and stability in Africa, and why both should be a main focus for U.S. military engagement on the continent.[2]

The only part of Bouchat's argument with which one might find fault regards whether good governance should be a primary focus for U.S. military engagement. While economic development through targeted education under the direction of the U.S. military is a likely gateway to good governance, the military should not engage in expensive and commonly unsuccessful anti-corruption programs currently and historically imposed on the nations of Sub-Saharan Africa.

We must look at Africa without our Western filter in order to understand it from a cultural and historical perspective. Today's nongovernmental organizations (NGOs) and other institutions gnash their teeth in frustration with corrupt African regimes. But transparency and the Western concept of good governance may not be the immediate priorities we think they should be. Perhaps these Western concepts and mechanisms must develop out of economic necessity and an indigenous desire within the construct of more robust economic systems that serve broader elements of society.

The Western view is that good governance and transparency are required **before** sustainable economic development can exist. However, it is more likely that training for the development of tangible assets within these countries will cause economic development to occur organically as people use those assets in ways intended or even unanticipated--such as using a poorly placed but newly paved road to dry tobacco leaves--to build up their own economic positions. Respect for property rights, contracts, and the rule of law developed in Western Europe over a period of centuries. Similarly, only when people gain economic success and interests worth protecting can they gradually evolve into a base that compels national governments to be responsive to their constituencies, thus imposing good governance from below.

On a continent so rich in mineral and oil resources, one of the vital missing elements of economic success is infrastructure. From the colonial powers' exploiting the region since the 17th century, to the Chinese seeking oil there in the 1970s, to the West's ravenous search for minerals today, roads and rails were built from the mine or the well to the port. These innovations were strictly for economic exploitation rather than as in Western Europe, connecting people internally, which likely would have prevented many of the post-independence battles over power and resources that still occur today.

Richard Dowden notes in his book, *Africa: Altered States, Ordinary Miracles* (2009):

> Africa's economies were twisted to serve Europe's needs. With the missionaries and colonial governors came the destruction of Africa's political systems, its culture, its dignity and self-worth. The brutal but brief conquest of Africa, particularly south of the Sahara, left it somehow stranded between tradition and Western modernity. . . . In Africa the European powers had been strong enough to destroy or subdue traditional African political systems but did not stay long enough to create new ones.[3]

In this conflict-prone region, national disarmament, demobilization, and reintegration (DDR) programs do not go far enough in providing vocational training for former military or paramilitary members. Despite the best efforts of well-meaning civil society and rule-of-law training, the overriding factor that emerges in keeping African ex-combatants from returning to the battlefield is jobs (individual and group post-traumatic therapy could greatly assist as well). But training for jobs is missing within African military establishments for those who will one day retire. Without jobs, they may otherwise resort to coups to maintain their status quo.

Therefore, rather than continuing to spend so much on post-conflict peacekeeping and nation rebuilding, focusing on creating opportunities and training programs leading to lucrative and status-maintaining civilian careers for serving African officers and noncommissioned officers (NCOs) is more likely to enhance the economic underpinnings of stability throughout the region. A number of African countries have military academies, but the vast majority of these teach only military sciences, not engineering or computer science, unlike, for example, West Point in the United States. When African officers and NCOs retire, all they know is soldiering.

Botswana is known in the region for its stability and relative economic opportunities. It is difficult not to connect this happy status with the fact that the majority of serving officers in the Botswana Defence Forces have completed U.S.-sponsored International Military Education and Training (IMET), billed as "a low cost, key funding component of U.S. security assistance." In addition to traditional military training, IMET graduates also receive instruction in "aviation safety . . . and [repair of] aircraft structure, fire control systems, avionics flight systems, and radio repair."[4]

Expanding on the IMET concept by establishing a single training facility in Africa would enable the U.S. military to provide engineering training to selected officers and NCOs. This could make an already low-cost program even less expensive as the early cohorts provide the trainers. Provision of engineering, telecommunications, and other valuable skills transferrable to the civilian economy would improve the discipline and loyalty of national service officers and NCOs. Use of this ready labor force to create a sustainable, functional infrastructure is also likely to attract needed private foreign investment.

Graduates will provide local expertise for infrastructure development, putting the tools in place for purely African solutions, without foreign entities determining the direction development should take. The African stakeholders themselves, in the form of governments, business interests, indigenous NGOs, and private investors, will identify the most pressing needs, develop the plans, create the supporting industries, and engage proactively in creating a future for Africa, without resorting to welfare state dependency resulting from aid-addicted budgets and corrupt regimes.

The Importance of Infrastructure to African Development.

According to a 2008 World Bank study, the lack of infrastructure in African nations diminishes business productivity by 40 percent. The largest infrastructure deficit is the inability to develop power and industrial sectors.[5] Once these fundamental gaps are filled, other aspects of African infrastructure can be expected to improve.

In conjunction with underdeveloped power industries, Africa writ large also lacks a unified road and rail infrastructure, which paralyzes its macro economies and divides the citizenry. However, at the regional and individual country level, the lack of physical infrastructure is also preventing growth and foreign investment needed to advance power and industrial sectors, and is ultimately limiting economic opportunity at the micro level, which leads to further instability.

As noted by Terry Dunmire, Corporate Council on Africa's (CCA) host to the U.S.-Africa Infrastructure Conference in Washington, DC, in July 2007:

> Infrastructure and its effectiveness and stability are the key skeletal structures on which the economies [of Africa] depend. It is the transportation systems that permit the goods and service to move effectively to

and from the markets; it is the telecommunications and IT [information technology] infrastructure that link the Continent with the rest of the world; it is the logistical systems that deliver products for all aspects of daily life; it is the electrical and power systems that make it run — in short, it is the efficiency and sufficiency of infrastructure that [are] essential to continued economic development in Africa.[6]

With regard to the value of using military resources to aid in infrastructure development, Adam Hochschild tells us in *King Leopold's Ghost* that even in the Congo in 1889:

[A]lmost all of Leopold's [Leopold II, King of the Belgians] agents in the Congo were officers on extended leave from the Belgian or other European armies. Staff in place and tools in hand, Leopold set out to build the infrastructure necessary to exploit his colony. A rudimentary Congo transportation system was the first item on his agenda, without it, the territory's riches, whatever they might turn out to be, could not be brought to the sea except on foot.[7]

But while Leopold wisely used military resources to build infrastructure, the infrastructure built was for the wrong purpose. Unfortunately, Leopold's scheme produced a prime example of much of the existing infrastructure across Sub-Saharan Africa. With very few exceptions, roads and railways, many of which have not seen significant improvements since the late 19th century, were built from mine to port, or merely served as a conduit for moving riches from the exploited colony to the mother country in Europe. They were not planned to move later commerce or to connect communities internally. This early pattern has perpetuated the divisive nature of tribalism and re-gionalism that so often degenerate into violent clashes to obtain economic potential for one's own, mainly in the form of land, natural resources, and labor.

This pattern is still being pursued with the majority of transportation and mining infrastructure rapidly built today by Chinese engineers in regions with valuable mineral and oil resources. It serves only the industries in which the Chinese firms have an interest, doing little to interconnect other commercial sectors and communities. In addition, indigenous jobs are not created by these projects, since the contracts go to Chinese firms that use their own labor resources.[8] Therefore, such infrastructural investments are unlikely to lead to long-term economic growth, either at the macro level for the country at large, or at the micro level for the benefit of individual African workers.

SUPPORT FOR INFRASTRUCTURE DEVELOPMENT AS KEY TO STABILITY

In the past, U.S. policymakers have tended to behave as patrons, treating each African country on a case-by-case basis by attempting to develop ties with individual leaders—using incentives such as food or other humanitarian or financial assistance and providing military training exercises and materiel. However, the United States has increasingly recognized Africa as the next front in the battle against radical Islam and as a strategic theater demanding a counterbalance against rising Chinese influence in the region. Thus, for America to provide practical education that can support African economic development is a logical approach.

The mandate of the newly established U.S. Africa Command (AFRICOM), requiring joint efforts of the U.S. Department of Defense (DoD) and the Department of State (DoS), is to enhance the development of professional, transparent, democratic, and appropriately tasked military institutions in African partner countries. It is instructive to note that U.S. policymakers, as well as Africans, have supported infrastructure as a key to this development. The AFRICOM 2009 *Posture Statement* notes the lack of infrastructure as a major factor "hindering states' efforts to develop in an ever-globalizing international environment."[9]

AFRICOM Commander General William "Kip" Ward's *Commander's Intent 2010* statement notes that:

> [O]ur national interests lie in a stable continent of Africa. This means that Africans live in the relative peace of a stable environment, are governed effectively, and enjoy a degree of economic and social advancement. An Africa whereby African populations are able to provide for themselves, contribute to global economic development, and allow access to markets in free, fair, and competitive ways, is good for America and for the world. . . . We will build partner security capacity in areas such as support and special staff capabilities, the African non-commissioned officer corps, and military/dual use infrastructures. . . . [10]

Prior to his appointment as AFRICOM Commander, General Ward declared in a November 14, 2007, interview on *The Charlie Rose Show* that he sees American forces in Africa "as facilitators, as trainers, as examples, as models, as forces for helping Africans be better prepared to increase their capacity to do their work."[11]

Before he even began his assignment as AFRICOM commander, Ward already knew what needed to be done. The Sub-Saharan region as a whole has not fully recovered from the shock of colonialism and the sudden onslaught of independence. Understanding this region as a body in the throes of post-traumatic stress, as opposed to a lagging developmental headache, provides us a better perspective for treating it in a holistic manner appropriate to its ills.

In a 2007 article entitled "Horizons of Hope," Ward discussed his experiences in three post-conflict operational environments, Somalia (1992), Bosnia (2000), and Palestine (2005):

> The United States and the international community must take the initiative to influence and rectify post-conflict situations before they become new fronts in the war on terror. . . . Unlike war plans that direct our own activities to achieve an objective, road maps recommend activities of the supported nation. Thus, they provide war-torn nations with plans and a direction that they themselves should embark upon. . . . The more situation-dependent implementation phase follows with the deliberate efforts to stabilize, reconstruct, and rebuild the country, concluding with the transition to an effective and stable society [which secures] the critical surviving infrastructure such as power grids, transportation networks, farmland, manufacturing, and other elements vital to the early reconstruction of the economy. . . . At the end of the implementation phase, the nation's economy is sufficiently self-sustaining that it can seek any further economic assistance on its own through standard international channels.[12]

By following Ward's own prescription, his Command can implement the U.S. Military Academy model as the road map for providing substantial and useful education to African military officers and NCOs, thus offering entire societies the opportunity to tap into their own structures and human resources to develop the tangible linkages necessary for sustained economic growth and a healthy body politic.

DoD Directive 3000.05, *U.S. Department of Defense, Military Support for Stability, Security, Transition, and Reconstruction (SSTR) Operations* (November 2005), establishes that it is DoD policy to "continue to support the development, implementation, and operations of civil-military teams and related efforts aimed at unity of effort in: rebuilding basic infrastructure; developing local governance structures; fostering security, economic stability, and development; and building indigenous capacity for such tasks."[13]

In their January 2010 Strategic Studies Institute (SSI) monograph, *Security Sector Reform: A Case Study Approach to Transition and Capacity Building,* Sarah Meharg and Aleisha Arnusch argue that stability requires a level of economic development that provides opportunities for the rising majority of currently idle and uneducated youth in Sub-Saharan African countries to participate in constructive activities. They further note that the U.S. Government's security sector reform (SSR) agenda is aligned with the goals of its partners, including:

> [M]embers of the OECD [Organisation for Economic Co-Operation and Development] view development and security as inextricably linked. . . . Security in all its dimensions is fundamental to reducing poverty, protecting human rights, and achieving UN Millennium Development Goals (MDGs)."[14]

The Millennium Challenge Corporation (MCC) Africa Infrastructure Fact Sheet states that "Poor infrastructure is an obstacle to private sector investment on the African continent, significantly driving up the cost of doing business, limiting new opportunities, and stunting economic growth.[15]

11

Additionally, research has shown strong links between improved infrastructure and poverty reduction, particularly in the areas of income, education, and health. As a result, the vast majority of countries eligible for Millennium Challenge Corporation funding have requested assistance in addressing local infrastructure needs. Among other initiatives, MCC projects include improvements to roads, bridges, energy facilities, water services, industries, and schools.[16]

Since the focus of this monograph is on Sub-Saharan Africa, it is appropriate to note what African leaders themselves have determined to be the critical infrastructure needs for economic development. This is clearly laid out in the New Partnership for Africa's Development (NEPAD) Strategic Framework, adopted at the 37th Summit of the Organisation for African Unity (OAU) in July 2001 as a program to create an integrated socioeconomic development framework for Africa. NEPAD's October 2001 report offers an initial road map that Ward said is so important for constructing or reconstructing these societies, including, "roads, highways, airports, seaports, railways, waterways, and telecommunications facilities."[17]

Western Aid Unsustainable Without Local Skills.

A recent *New York Times* article referred to the Ethiopian village of Koraro as "an important testing ground for the Millennium Village Project (MVP), an experiment in global development strategy spearheaded by economist Jeffrey Sachs." This case underscores the need to create the indigenous human capital that Africa needs to develop. "I think the sustainability of the project is a real problem," notes Robert Chase, a World Bank Economist and Human Development

Sector Leader in Ethiopia. "How you're going to pull out and expect the economic growth to continue is not immediately clear to me."

The article noted that others

> question the team's ability to scale the project up to the hundreds of millions of people stuck in extreme poverty, cringing at the additional billions of dollars that would need to be spent and the army of well-trained, highly-educated managers that would need to be identified.

It further notes that

> one MVP employee who has worked at multiple Millennium Villages (and wished to remain anonymous) said that the local project coordinators—people with significant development experience and ties to the region—are few and far between. Finding similarly-qualified people to liaise with every single village throughout the poverty-stricken world, he believes, is a long shot.[18]

Stella Kagwanja, a Kenyan woman from the Kamba tribe, said recently at a U.S. Army Culture Center event, "You know, Africans have a collective culture, once you teach something to one person, you have taught a whole village, because they will go home and teach everyone what they have learned." Kagwanja went on to say that:

> Everyone worries about all this tribalism. This is not an important issue in reality, because if the Kamba or the Luo see the Kikuyu doing something or having something like a new road or a power station in their lands, they will work to make sure they have one too. This is also the beauty of building infrastructure, who cares if the Kikuyu are getting all the funding

now for new roads, for instance, once the roads are there, everyone can use them, not only the Kikuyu or whomever built them. Once they are there, everybody benefits.[19]

As noted in a recent *Philadelphia Enquirer* article, "The Joint Chiefs Chairman, Admiral Mike Mullen, travelled to the opening of one of the Central Asia Institute's (CAI's) Afghan schools, and later told an American Legion convention: 'We cannot capture hearts and minds. We must engage them; we must listen to them'."[20]

U.S. civilian officials have been slower to grasp the need to confer more with locals and find it harder to do because of security considerations. CAI Director Greg Mortenson says if they did sit down with *shuras* (councils of local elders), they would understand that what Afghans want most is training, whether in regular schools, or vocational or agricultural courses. Rather than use big contractors, he says, we must teach the Afghans themselves to do the job.[21]

The same can clearly be said of Africans individually, and of the Sub-Saharan region generally, that is otherwise likely to become prey to extremist ideologies. Such training in this region, even in its genesis, is likely to head off many of the problems that U.S. Central Command (CENTCOM) is now fighting to contain and eliminate. Why not train in-country for the skills needed? Why have to scour Western universities, as is currently happening, for qualified engineers, project managers, and development experts at prohibitive costs, when they could be found among African military officers and NCOs seeking a useful transition to civilian life?

AFRICAN MILITARIES: SUPPORTERS OR DESTABILIZERS?

Meharg and Arnusch assert that:

> Peace spoilers are a source of risk during peace and
> stability operations, in particular to SSR activities.
> Spoilers are nonstate actors that can be individual
> leaders as well as organizations that believe the sta-
> bility emerging from intervention threatens their
> power, worldview, cultural identities, and interests,
> and therefore they will use techniques to undermine
> attempts to achieve stable outcomes.[22]

In Sub-Saharan Africa, historical precedent requires this list of spoilers to be expanded to include
serving members of national military organizations,
who undermine stability by installing spoiler leaders
as in Zimbabwe; and members who choose to participate in military coups and insurgencies, as in Nigeria,
Somalia, and elsewhere.

William Tordoff in his book, *Government and Politics in Africa*, includes an entire chapter on the causes
of military coups:

a. Factionalism: including tribalism, elitism, re-
gionalism, and the cultural mandate that, once in
power of any kind, it is your responsibility to ensure
that your group monopolizes the economic trough.
We note, however, that as the national supply increas-
es, the dipping into the till diminishes.

b. Ideology: radicalism among the ruling elite or
military elite. When there is constructive work to be
had and done, and enough to go around, the attrac-
tion of radicalism is reduced.

c. Threat to military corporate interests. Further
educating and professionalizing the military officer
and NCO corps is likely to create a mirroring effect

by later expanding the new middle class that will ultimately ensure that the rulers are responsible to the taxpaying electorate, thus increasing stability and accountability in all facets of society. Secure pay and benefits for military retirees and those in active service will reinforce this beneficial effect.

d. Personal Issues. Providing opportunities for ex-military in the civilian sector diminishes turf battles and the need to protect one's own interests at the expense of society.[23]

Providing widespread economic opportunity within society, especially for army officers and NCOs when they separate from service, is likely to diminish greatly the pressures of these underlying causes.

As Nigeria has been the most coup-prone and corrupt of the region's states since independence, it is not surprising that it has a poor record of caring for its retired military. At the very least, ensuring retirement payments should be a priority. In December 2009, the new Chairman of the Military Pensions Board (MPB), Brigadier General BVT Kwaji, reported on the military pension plan in place by law since 2004. He found that the Pension Reform Act had not improved the problem of irregular pay for military retirees.[24]

A 2009 *allAfrica* article praised Kwaji's efforts to improve the situation, stating, "Before his arrival, it was almost seen as a luxury to extend pension and gratuity to retired and discharged members of the country's military force, who had put their lives on the line to defend the land."[25] Encouraging those currently serving to pursue education that would provide economic opportunity upon separation is likely to prevent additional military coups and improve Nigeria's poor infrastructure, thus removing some of the financial burden on the state, which has thus far failed to provide its pledged support.

Some countries in the region are making military education a priority and striving to use it as a resource to grow their economic opportunities across society. Botswana and Somaliland, for example, are focused on the value of education, seeing the military as an important component of stability. Nigeria is a negative example, demonstrating how *not* to invest effectively in infrastructure.

Botswana: "What Africa Might Have Become."

Botswana has not experienced violence, nor has it required DDR programs. It is commonly held up as the prime example of what can go right in Sub-Saharan Africa. It must be noted that although there is a minority population of Bushmen who still live in the traditional mode, they do not directly interact with the majority Botswana population, which is largely homogeneous and a strong factor in the country's stability. Botswana is an example of the effective use of an African military to safeguard national infrastructure. In his book, *Africa: Altered States, Ordinary Miracles* (2009), Richard Dowden notes, "Botswana's elected government spent the money [from diamond revenues] on giving its people improved education and health and better roads and water. Visiting Botswana makes you realize what all of Africa might have become."[26]

The Botswana Defence Forces (BDF) are often hailed as a model professional military, with 30 officers a year participating in U.S. Army IMET training.[27] Analysts have described the BDF as having high standards of discipline, an emphasis on education, and competent leadership at all levels. Reflecting awareness of the need for an effective selection and admissions policy for U.S.-sponsored training efforts, the BDF starts "with good human material. It is very selective in recruitment of its personnel and education plays a key role in personnel selection and career progression."[28]

The BDF sends many officers to study in South Africa and overseas, with a Jane's estimate in 2004 that "75% of BDF officers above the rank of major are graduates of U.S. military schools." According to Dan Henk's interview in the same year with Lieutenant Colonel P. T. F. Sharp, BDF Director of Career Development and Training:

> The minimum educational qualification for an officer candidate is a Cambridge A-level "first class pass" and half of the officer candidates selected for BDF service have university degrees. Enlisted recruits must at a minimum possess a Cambridge O-level certification. Many of the successful enlisted applicants have additional trade school or apprenticeship training as well.[29]

In 2007, Henk detailed the effectiveness of the BDF as an instrument of positive growth in his book, *The Botswana Defence Force in the Struggle for an African Environment*, which highlights the state's use of its Army. Such uses include safeguarding the country's unique but vulnerable wildlife. By ensuring Botswana's status as a stable and secure nation in the region, the army helps the country to remain a safari tourist destination. The economic benefits of that industry are considerable, accounting for 12 percent of the gross domestic product (GDP) in 2008.[30]

Somaliland: Opting Out of Civil War by Building Capacity.

Somaliland is a republic within Somalia, having declared its independence from British rule in 1960 but eventually agreeing to a partnership with Puntland and Somalia. However, once violence overtook those regions in 1991, the Somaliland Congress voted to reinstate its independent status. Since that time, despite the fact that no country has recognized its secession, it has managed to maintain relative security and stability, even prosecuting 15 pirates that Somaliland's own Navy had caught in its territorial waters in December 2009.[31]

Interestingly, this unrecognized, poverty-stricken republic managed to create the Berbera Maritime College in 2005. This college, claiming to follow International Maritime Bureau (IMB) standards, is the training ground for the Somaliland Navy, with over 100 officers specifically trained to fight pirates off the 450 mile-long Somaliland coast. The idea of forming a robust Somali Coast Guard both to prevent piracy and to provide jobs for former pirates willing to forsake their current profession has been proposed by a number of international organizations and individuals, but rather than waiting for the world to act on the idea, Somaliland has gotten to work on its own.

The College's business plan notes that despite the fishing industry's potential as an economic driver, it contributes less than 1 percent to the nation's gross national product (GNP). This is due to the "lack of adequate fishing equipment, on-shore facilities, skilled personnel, commercial organisation, public policy, and cultural orientation." The college claims to be the first in the country to address these issues, aiming to take a leading role "in the development of the national marine economy by providing professional and vocational skill training programs for secondary school [drop-outs], fishermen as well as ship and port operators." It also aims to become a prominent marine research and resource center, which will undertake studies on marine resources, the environment, and commercial development.[32]

The course curriculum includes a full offering of science and mathematics courses, as well as English language and courses focused on port maintenance, the fishing industry, and marine ecology as promised. Although its website indicates a long "wish list" of materials, equipment, and even instructors needed, this is a critical effort to provide vocational training within both the civilian and military contexts so as to develop the knowledge and infrastructure for a sustainable economic sector. Without international recognition, Somaliland is ineligible for international aid; therefore, it is attempting to use education and its own Navy to develop expertise and infrastructure to take advantage of existing resources for development.

Nigeria: What NOT to Do.

The Niger Delta Development Commission (NDDC) was established in 2000, in recognition of the marginalization and environmental degradation caused since the 1950s in the Delta and the increasingly poor conditions of those living there as oil profits are siphoned off in Nigeria's rampant corruption. In an attempt to end the violence in the region, the NDDC has initiated a number of localized infrastructure projects, including electrification, canals, roads, bridges, water systems, schools, and hospitals. The

NDDC notes that its "[s]kills acquisition program is designed to train youths in vocational skills in various trades such as pipefitting, welding, automobile and river craft repairs, electrical/electronics. . . . The rationale is to create more jobs for youths with a view to making them self-reliant." The latest NDDC data show that a total of 6,070 youths have benefited from the skills-acquisition program. A survey conducted by the Commission showed that most of the beneficiaries are either "self-employed or gainfully employed in private institutions."[33]

This is progress of a sort, but it is notable that so few have been trained and that these students are self-employed when they could be building the infrastructure the program has mandated as its goal. As recently as February 18, 2010, the Nigerian House of Representatives passed a bill recommending that "all operators and alliance partners . . . maintain a bidding process for acquiring goods and services which shall give full and fair opportunity to Nigerian indigenous contractors and companies." The bill further states that "qualified Nigerians shall be given first consideration for training and employment in work programmes for which the plan was submitted."[34] This bill was passed nearly 10 years after the NDDC Act went into effect. Most egregiously, the lawmakers only belatedly (2009) recognized that "operators should train Nigerians in the areas Nigerians were not [qualified for] in oil and gas contracts due to lack of requisite experience and qualification."[35]

An October 2009 BBC report on the progress of Nigeria's current demobilization of Movement for the Emancipation of the Niger Delta (MEND) militants notes:

Until now, they have lived in militant camps, carrying out kidnappings, blowing up oil pipelines and stealing massive amounts of crude oil. What happens to these men now is crucial to the future of the Delta. Already there have been street protests in Yenagoa, in Bayelsa State, by youths angry at not receiving money they had been promised in return for dumping guns. The government says it will take these young men and re-train them—sponsoring them through education to learn new skills or trades. But if the promises of a better future are broken, it is likely they will return to violence.[36]

The Nigerian authorities are only beginning the process of interviewing these young men at transitional centers to determine what kind of training they want and need. The next questions include who will provide and fund the program, and will society accept them in their chosen trades if they actually obtain the promised education? Bonny Gaeei, a young leader who induced the 260 former MEND members under his command to turn in their weapons, said, "I trust them, I must trust them. They, the government, they have every power. Let them do as they say. If they don't? Then, I will bust pipelines again. That is the truth."[37]

Nigeria has the capacity to make good on these promises with its proven oil reserves and the many jobs this industry should have been providing for Nigerians since the 1950s. However, the government has succumbed to the "Dutch Disease," that is, failing to develop the industry as a national asset for economic growth, but rather as a cash cow for elites. Today, only a small percentage of those employed in Nigeria's oil and gas industry are Nigerian.

Augustine Ikelegbe described the negative effects of the mismanagement of oil revenues in the Delta in a 2006 *African and Asian Studies* article, noting that the economy of conflict has destroyed the traditional cohesive culture and replaced it with new values. These new values only help private interests, and lead to disrespect for elders and traditional systems. Ikelegbe says that they have also created a "macho, might is right, cultist and violent culture. Productive labor has been disdained in the context of cheap oil fallouts and handouts."[38]

There is a widespread understanding that DDR, including a universal appreciation for education as a basis for economic growth, is an important aspect of post-conflict civil-society building. However, implementation tends to be the sticking point.

In the popular book *Three Cups of Tea* (2006), there is a poignant scene between the author, Greg Mortenson, and an Afghan warlord, Sadhar Khan. Mortenson notes that Khan routinely collected "tolls" from opium traffickers crossing his fiefdom and used the funds to help his people in Baharak, Northern Afghanistan, by building a huge bazaar and extending loans to his men to set up lucrative shops once they laid down their arms. Khan commented to Mortenson that all the stones they saw in the valley below the roof of the building on which they stood represented Khan's fallen soldiers, his *mujahedeen*, and asked Mortenson to turn all these stones into schools as a monument to their sacrifice.[39]

A 2007 UNDP report assessing the effectiveness of DDR programs in Africa asserts, "[O]f those emerging states that have relapsed into conflict since the end of the cold war, the failure of DDR has contributed, either directly or indirectly, to the outbreak of approximately 60% of these armed conflicts."[40] The common factor in all these experiences is the clear understanding that one-time payoffs, individual therapy, and civil society training are not enough to dissuade potential spoilers from causing further instability.

The critical factor for success is providing skills training that can ensure viable employment in infrastructure creation and maintenance for individual and societal development. While the training may be provided by foreign entities, the participants self-select for the skill-sets most appropriate to the domestic economy, matching those needed for building the infrastructure that will lead to sustainable overall economic development. In Nigeria, the focus would initially be on professions associated with the oil and gas industry; in Liberia, the timber industry; and so on.

In the final phase of post-conflict DDR, reintegration, only the very basic aspects of education are addressed in most cases, as noted by Massimo Fusato in a 2003 article describing the processes and requirements of successful DDR:

> Economic integration is the final requirement for a DDR program to be successful and sustainable in the long term. The goal of economic reintegration efforts is to provide ex-combatants with financial independence through employment. . . . Common economic integration programs include education and professional training, public employment, encouragement of private initiative through skills development and microcredit support, and access to land.[41]

Only the most cursory attention to education and professional training is made in most cases, and Fusato notes that cash payments in place of training tend to be favored for ex-combatants. However, their effectiveness has not been proven as a long-term strategy. As stated by Mr. Francis Kai-Kai, who headed Sierra Leone's national DDR committee, "You don't just focus on men and weapons, but on their futures as well."[42]

As attested by a review of a number of African DDR cases, vocational training emerges as the greatest single indicator of success. However, rather than rewarding combatants who have destabilized central governments, this review advocates rewarding those in the national military who are currently serving to support and maintain central government stability. The primary participants should be those who have done their duty and deserve the skills needed to achieve success when they separate. At that time, they are able to combine those infrastructure-developing skills with the discipline and desire to continue to serve their nation.

The point of this monograph is not necessarily to suggest that the intent of training African officers and NCOs as engineers while they are in the military is for them to perform that duty while in the service. But a case might be made, in some instances, for creating a separate serving corps for infrastructure development along the lines of the U.S. Army Corps of Engineers, as Botswana has done.

EDUCATION AND TRAINING MODELS FOR AFRICAN MILITARY ACADEMIES

The need in Sub-Saharan Africa is for trained engineers of various types to spearhead infrastructure development as civilian actors, whether employed by their own civil administrations or local or international NGOs, or in private practice with local capital or through foreign direct investment. Engineering training is not needed only in African militaries, but the military provides the necessary structure and the discipline for developing this capacity. Moreover, it is an arena in which U.S. partnership is uniquely suited. The added benefit of improving civil-military relations as a result of visible infrastructure projects is likely to further enhance stability in the region.

Except for South Africa, the Botswanan, Kenyan, and Tanzanian militaries have the most advanced military academies in Sub-Saharan Africa and provide training for their own and for other African countries' service personnel. However, based on these nations' institutions, it is evident that the current model of military academies in Africa is that of a liberal arts education with a focus on humanities. While this approach is understandable, given the current role of African militaries in peacekeeping and humanitarian missions, it likely does little to benefit post-military careers or to create the skills needed for national economic development.[43]

The lack of infrastructure development in Africa is not strictly a military problem; however, the model of the U.S. Army Corp of Engineers (CoE) and the U.S. armed services engineering components indicates that having the military involved in infrastructure development and maintenance is likely an efficient strategy.

There are myriad historical examples of critical infrastructure development, both domestic and overseas, where these U.S. military-engineering organizations have participated. More specifically, U.S. Army CoE, as part of the Military Civic Action (MCA), operated in Africa from 1985 to 1995, working to build up civil capabilities. The goal of the program was to demonstrate to African militaries the usefulness of building facilities for civilians as a method to improve civil-military relations and civil-military trust.[44]

The program was extremely successful in improving civil opinion of the military; however, U.S. engineers provided all the technical expertise. The United States supplied all of the technical engineering assistance in project evaluation, planning, and cost estimates; site surveys; logistical advice; implementation oversight; and a limited amount of equipment procurement, materials, and spare parts.[45] Consequently, once each individual project was complete, the host nation was left with no residual capability to duplicate its success.

While the majority of U.S. Army CoE personnel are not military officers, the leader of the organization is, and the organization has a clear military affiliation and atmosphere.[46] Additionally, the United States has built an engineering component into each of its services with many certified engineers serving as junior and senior officers.

This capability is not only combat effective; it also provides vital skills, training, and educational opportunities to individual officers once their military service is complete. According to a 1999 report, the U.S. military and government employed over 110,000 engineers combined, whereas the private sector employed 1.3 million. However, engineers employed in the private sector tended to be older by 4 years on average, and private sector employers tend to favor applicants with proven job experience gained through military engineering service.[47]

The importance of engineering and technical skills to the U.S. military is evident in the curriculum of the U.S. military service academies, particularly West

Point. Every cadet attending the academy must take a minimum of four math, two chemistry, two information technology, two physics, and three engineering courses as part of the basic curriculum.

Additionally, cadets can choose to major in one of only three tracks: engineering, science, or humanities. According to West Point's own data, approximately 45 percent of students choose to focus on engineering or science. Within the engineering program, the Academy offers six specific accredited programs: civil engineering, electrical engineering, engineering management, environmental engineering, mechanical engineering, and systems engineering.[48] In addition to West Point, the other service academies have similarly strong engineering and science traditions.[49]

In contrast, African militaries and military academies lack the engineering education and training available to U.S. officers. The Kenyan military academy, for example, does not offer any engineering programs, and the only relevant courses offered are in basic mathematics and computer use. However, the Kenyan Army Electrical and Mechanical Engineering specialty is similar to the engineering Military Occupation Specialty in the U.S. Army. The Kenyan Air Force does offer engineering programs and degree opportunities to future officers that are likely to be of an extremely high caliber.[50] However, it is still the only service with an engineering training capability, which is used only in narrowly operational roles within the military and is compartmentalized within the air force.[51]

While it is likely that a transition to a science and technology focused military academy system based on the U.S. West Point model would greatly benefit African militaries, the Chinese model of officer placement in civil service and infrastructure development projects is also a possible model to increase civil-military stability in Africa. If a Kenyan officer retires prior to the age of 55, he or she must remain in a reserve capacity.[52] In contrast, officers who retire at any age from the Chinese military are funneled into civil service. Over the last 60 years, the Chinese government estimates that over 4 million former officers have been assigned jobs working on civil service projects building Chinese infrastructure in both rural and urban areas.[53]

The Chinese model thus instills a lifelong dedication to and investment in the country by its military officers (we must admit that opportunities for some usurpation of state resources serve as an additional incentive), making it unlikely that officers would want to undermine the country's stability. This principle was underscored by Chinese Vice President Xi Jinping's statement that officers "carry on a good tradition in the army, maintain loyalty to the party, and continue working for the country's development and stability."[54] By applying the Chinese model in conjunction with a well-trained engineering corps, African governments would be able to build capacity in former officers to develop the infrastructure of the nation, foster continued loyalty to the nation, and remove an incentive to participate in coups or other destabilizing activities.

In conjunction with the improvement of officer education and placement, it is highly likely that the development of a job-placement program for enlisted soldiers and NCOs would greatly improve civil-military relations. In conjunction with the data from other cases noted above, from 1992 to 1995, Uganda conducted a large demobilization. However, there were clear failures to provide post-military workshops, a drought coincidentally created unexpected agricultural strains, housing and residency issues arose for displaced veterans, and all but the most conspicuously qualified veterans lacked marketable skills and thus money to live. Accordingly, the general public became fearful of the veterans' presence in society.[55]

For correcting these problems, a 2001 monograph by the South African-based Institute for Security Studies recommends that prior to any demobilization, governments plan for transition by the following steps: (1) create social networks to help integrate and transition soldiers back into civilian society; (2) provide them with information and training; (3) alert domestic firms of the skills soldiers offer to private industry; (4) provide vouchers for technical training; (5) encourage involvement in civil service; and (6) create systems to monitor veterans. These recommendations mirror the U.S. Army Program for Youth Success (PaYS) system, which is designed to provide an all-source resource center for job placement and career training for Cadets and enlisted personnel as well as a source for finding qualified applicants for private industry positions.[56]

A 2007 Bureau of Labor Statistics article, "Military Training for Civilian Careers," in *Occupational Outlook Quarterly*, points out that the unemployment rate for veterans tends to be lower than that of the general U.S. labor force. In August 2005, the unemployment rate was 3.6 percent for veterans and 4.9 percent overall. The article continues:

> The military trains you to be technically proficient in whatever occupation you are assigned. But you'll also learn teamwork, perseverance, leadership, and other skills widely applicable in the civilian workforce. In fact, some employers looking for workers with specific qualifications . . . often seek out former military personnel.

Most armed-services jobs have a direct civilian counterpart. If you learn how to repair and maintain vehicles, for example, you might later use these skills as a mechanic in the civilian world. . . . And if you learn to maintain military computer systems, you might find civilian work as a computer specialist. In the military, you'll earn career credentials. You'll also have a chance to further your education while you serve--and afterward.[57]

The economic climate of 2008-2010 has not been as kind to American veterans returning from Afghanistan and Iraq as it was in 2005. However, developing an African-based training program could employ a number of currently displaced veterans with the requisite health and skills.

THE MILITARY ACADEMY MODEL AND ITS APPLICABILITY TO AFRICA

Developing U.S.-style military academies in Sub-Saharan Africa to educate military officers and NCOs who might otherwise engage in destructive or destabilizing activities due to a lack of economic opportunity, is a long-term stabilization effort. Providing such positive opportunities for economic and status advancement is critical within the context of a basic and widespread lack of lucrative post-retirement employment opportunity, particularly in post-conflict DDR situations.

To enhance stability in Sub-Saharan Africa, military officers need to be given incentives to remain loyal, professional, and disciplined. As the Nigerian case illustrates, retiree payments are not always reliable, a situation made worse by loss of status when one leaves the military. Therefore, instituting a civilian career path for current and future officers and NCOs, as Botswana, China, the United States, and many other professional military organizations have done, is likely to have a salutary effect.

It is clear that a lack of education and infrastructure underlie the low level of economic development that leads to poverty and violence in Sub-Saharan Africa. The greatest hindrance to building the infrastructure Africa needs for economic development and stability — whether it is for transportation, communication, power generation, or water sanitation and irrigation — is not only lack of material resources, but lack of human capital. This region lacks the massive numbers of engineers and project managers needed to plan, design, develop, implement, and maintain the projects most critical to national and regional development.

Development professionals like to talk about African solutions for African problems. Without the requisite education, however, it is nearly impossible for Africans to develop or implement optimum solutions to the continent's problems. Since its inception in October 2008, AFRICOM has provided valuable military-to-military training to a number of African partners. However, a long-term strategy should focus on creating a holistic approach to professionalizing military service as a part of members' lives and as an avenue to greater economic development efforts upon separation from the service.

The larger objective of building a critical mass of skills necessary for designing, building, and maintaining essential infrastructure must include the intermediate objective of creating a train-the-trainer curriculum lending itself to the ultimate development of a cadre of African instructors who can continually reassess the requirements and conduct the training of future skilled African military officers and NCOs.

U.S.-style military academies offer the best venue. Such academies are highly likely to engender a cycle of professional services and opportunity development to stem the current brain drain leading educated and ambitious African civilians to abandon their own land for opportunities abroad. Such an academy initiative is also likely to provide educational and advancement opportunities to former service members, thus discouraging them from seeking less constructive employment pathways for themselves at the expense of the larger society.

RECOMMENDATIONS FOR IMPLEMENTATION

How to develop curricula, staffing, and an admissions program for professional-skills military academies in Sub-Saharan Africa is beyond the scope of this monograph. However, some recommendations can be made based on the current body of research and an appreciation of African conditions. The first recommendation is to create an initial pair of state-of-the-art academies, one for officers and one for NCOs. The second recommendation is to train cadets (and later officers) to become engineers in such specialties as energy, electrical, industrial, hydro, mechanical, mining, and petrochemical. The third recommendation relates to NCOs, who are the subject matter experts and teachers of junior enlisted service members. They must be taught leadership and managerial skills, as well as mechanical; bridge, airport and port facility management; power station maintenance; and water irrigation, reclamation, or sanitation plant-building and maintenance skills. Their academies must ensure that these skills are developed. The specific skill-set targets for both schools should be dictated by partner-led needs assessments.

The location of these two academies should be determined in discussion with partner nations, but consideration could be given to placing the officer training academy in Botswana in recognition of its good governance and maintenance of a high standard of military discipline. The new Botswana Defence Command College is projected to be completed at Glen Valley by the end of 2011, which may serendipitously offer an initial location for hosting parts of the program. Once that institution is operational, the academy could move into the college's present (interim) location, which opened in January 2008 near the capital, Gabarone.[58]

Similarly, after negotiation with U.S. partners, the NCO Academy could be placed in Tanzania as an incentive to ward off rising Islamic extremist influence and to further support Tanzania in its struggle to reform its armed forces along Western lines, from the traditional socialist structure it now bears. The country has not fought a war since its 1979 invasion of Uganda and is thus not battle-ready. It would therefore be unable to defend itself or respond to any emergencies caused by militant Islamists. Tanzania is not radicalized, merely weak, and a strong show of U.S. support for developing the Tanzanian military with a defensive orientation is a particular opportunity for AFRICOM to display the partnership aspect of its mission.[59]

As telecommunications infrastructure expands in the region, a longer-term plan should include locations for distance education to supplement hands-on training so as to increase enrollment and reduce staffing and overall costs.

The arbitrary division of African territory that took place under colonialism forcibly separated historical lands, tribes, and even families into artificial "nations" that have not entirely taken hold in Sub-Saharan Africa in the post-colonial period. To overcome the issues of tribalism and to prevent preferential treatment of some tribes over others in developing the human capital needed to build critical infrastructure across the region, we should consider creating the academies under the auspices of the Southern African Development Community.

An SSI study by Dr. Steven Metz, *Refining American Strategy in Africa* (2000), observes that African culture places a "great value" on collective action, and that "the most tangible gains have come from building on existing structures."[60] A great shortcoming of Western policy in Africa and elsewhere throughout modern history is an assumption that we are working with a blank slate upon which we can impose our own plans and methods, thus failing to recognize the significance of existing cultural values, beliefs, behaviors, and norms. Working within this preexisting framework can reduce friction and enhance collaboration and acceptance of new concepts and processes. The existing and emerging cooperative structures within the African Union and subregional organizations provide a viable platform upon which to provide assistance toward needed reforms.

This approach should be considered within the context of inviting active South African participation in curriculum development and staffing, so as not to appear to be attempting to usurp the influential role this country currently plays as a regional military training center. South Africa is also likely to have the human resources to cut down on the number of U.S.

and European faculty needed from the outset. The approach is likely to have the added benefit of enhancing U.S.-South African relations within a partnership for regional success, rather than a patronage relationship.

As Metz has observed, "The African security environment may be the most complex on earth, with a sometimes bewildering array of actors, shifting affiliations, and unique characteristics."[61] All of these factors are potentially destabilizing and must be first understood, then accommodated, when designing engagement strategy. The personalization of power requires long-term U.S. strategic engagement, rather than the historical norm of providing short-term support to particular rulers as they fit into the scheme du jour of U.S. or European national interest. However, Metz further notes that African leaders have recognized that "the region's internal conflicts are extraordinarily complex and often expensive in both blood and money."[62] Mutual understanding of this fact is likely to be an excellent basis for positive engagement.

Determining the training programs most optimal for sustained development in the region is a critical part of the planning of the two academies, and must be conducted with input from local authorities and experts, who can ensure that the skills training meets the most critical skills requirements. Too often Western assistance is directed toward programs that appear logical in Washington or Brussels, but have little relevance to the situation on the ground in Africa.

By the same token, the goal of the recommended program is to create a local pool of trained engineers and skilled laborers who can accomplish the infrastructure design and development tasks required most for sustained economic development and growth in the region over the long term. It is critical that the program keep in sight that singular goal—avoiding any so-called "mission creep" toward such secondary goals as establishing transparency in government, or ending corruption, or any other ultimately desirable outcome. Though desirable, these goals must come later as by-products of sustained and widespread economic opportunity and growth.

The author, a former member of International Monetary Fund mission teams, arrived at these conclusions through extensive research on the current U.S. military training that is intended to prepare service members for civilian occupations; on DDR programs; on U.S. and African convictions on the critical need for infrastructure creation as the key to sustainable economic development; and on their conclusions as to what has gone right and wrong in Africa toward achieving these goals in the decades since independence.

When considering planning for a military-to-military training program that will diminish the likelihood of a military coup or further instability in the target country, the recommendations set forth in Dr. Donovan Chau's SSI Monograph, *U.S. Counterterrorism in Sub-Saharan Africa: Understanding Costs, Cultures, and Conflicts* (2008), are clearly valid:

> [T]he USG [U.S. Government] [should] think long-term continually, build meaningful relationships in SSA [Sub-Saharan Africa], move counterterrorism beyond DoD-centric operations, and, most importantly, educate future analysts, officers, and policymakers about the African continent. What should be borne in mind throughout, and is often lost in the U.S. policy-making process, is that foreign governments and peoples do not often view the world according to Western liberal values, attitudes, and beliefs. This is as true in counterterrorism as it is in any other strategic issue. [63]

Ensuring equitable admission to the academies in terms of merit, as opposed to tribal or other forms of patronage, is the purview of those tasked to set up the schools and not within the scope of this monograph. However, ensuring meritorious matriculation of the best and brightest students most likely to succeed in their studies is paramount in achieving the success of this initiative.

The United States can assist in designing methods to identify the up-and-coming leaders who may be only on the periphery now. They will become the new generation of African leaders with a fresh perspective—those who may have spent time abroad, those who understand that the rule of law and the development of a stable middle class have longer-term benefits for the security of all, and those who reject the traditional corrupt practices that have bankrupted most African countries.

As Philip Neikerk has cogently argued:

> Africa's hope for leadership is a younger generation that for now remains on the margins. The sooner a new wave of leaders is able to exert power and moral direction, the better placed the continent will be to mediate its own problems and ward off outside interference. Until then, the dinosaurs rule.[64]

ENDNOTES

1. Project Gutenberg's *The History of Rome*, Books 01 to 08, by Titus Livius, D. Spillan, A.M. M.D., trans. and annotated, London, UK: Henry G. Bohn, 1853, p. 194, para. 29, available from *www.gutenberg.org/files/19725/19725-h/19725-h.htm*.

2. Clarence J. Bouchat, *Security And Stability In Africa: A Development Approach*, Carlisle, PA: Strategic Studies Institute, U.S. Army War College, 2010, p. vii, available from *www.strategicstudiesinstitute.army.mil/pubs/display.cfm?pubID=964*.

3. Richard Dowden, *Africa: Altered States, Ordinary Miracles,* New York: Public Affairs, 2009, pp. 55-56.

4. International Military Education and Training (IMET) page, Defense Security Cooperation Agency (DCSA) web site, July 21, 2010, available from *www.dsca.mil/home/international_military_ education_training.htm.*

5. Vivien Foster, "Overhauling the Engine of Growth: Infrastructure in Africa," *Africa Infrastructure Country Diagnostic* (AICD), Washington, DC: World Bank, September 2008, available from *siteresources.worldbank.org/INTAFR:ICA/Resources/AICD_exedc_ summ_9-30-08a.pdf.*

6. Erik Arnetz, Interview with Terry Dunmire, the Director of Business Development of DynCorp International (DI), while Dunmire hosted the *Building On Stability – The U.S.-Africa Infrastructure Conference* in Washington, DC, on July 28, 2007, published in *Africa Journal,* available from *craigeisele.wordpress.com/2007/09/02/ building-on-stability-the-us-africa-infrastructure-conference/;* Derek Reveron, "Africa Command: Security and Stability, Not Oil or Confrontation," Council for Emerging National Security Affairs (CENSA) Notes, February 2007, available from *www.censa.net/ AfricaCommand_DReveron.pdf.*

7. Adam Hochschild, *King Leopold's Ghost: A Story of Greed, Torture, and Heroism in Colonial Africa,* New York: First Mariner Books, 1999, pp. 90-91.

8. Eugene Bawelle, "China-Africa relations, any benefits?" *Modern Ghana: Business and Finance,* available from *www. modernghana.com/news/254412/1/china-africa-relations-any-benefits. html.*

9. "United States Africa Command Posture Statement 2009," March 2009, available from *www.africom.mil/getArticle. asp?art=4133&lang=0.*

10. General William "Kip" Ward, "United States Africa Command Commander's Intent 2010," available from *www.africom. mil/pdfFiles/Commander%27s%20Intent%20January%202010.pdf.*

11. Interview with General William "Kip" Ward by Charlie Rose, The Charlie Rose Show, November 17, 2007, available from *www.charlierose.com/view/interview/8779.*

12. See *www.ndu.edu/inss/Press/jfq_pages/editions/i45/12.pdf.*

13. "Stability Operations," *U.S. Department of Defense Instruction Number 3000.05,* Washington, DC: Department of State, September 16, 2009, available from *www.dtic.mil/whs/directives/corres/ pdf/300005p.pdf.*

14. Sarah Meharg and Aleisha Arnusch, *Security Sector Reform: A Case Study Approach to Transition and Capacity Building,* Carlisle, PA: Strategic Studies Institute, U.S. Army War College, 2010, available from *www.strategicstudiesinstitute.army.mil/pubs/ display.cfm?pubID=960.*

15. "MCC Infrastructure Programs in African Countries," Millennium Challenge Corporation Fact Sheet, April 8, 2008, available from *www.mcc.gov/documents/press/factsheet-040808-africa-infrastructure.pdf.*

16. *Ibid.*

17. *New Partnership for Africa's Development,* October 2001, pp. 22-23, available from *www.nepad.org/images/framework.pdf.*

18. Nicholas D. Kristof, "Kararo: The Sustainability Factor," *New York Times: On the Ground,* January 27, 2010, available from *kristof.blogs.nytimes.com/2010/01/27/koraro-the-sustainability-factor/.*

19. Stella Kagwanja, Kenyan native and former USAID subcontractor in Nairobi now residing in Sierra Vista, AZ, conversation with author, February 21, 2010.

20. *Ibid.*

21. Trudy Rubin, "Worldview: A Surge in Schools," *The Philadelphia Inquirer,* January 17, 2010, available from: *www.philly.com/ inquirer/columnists/trudy_rubin/20100117_Worldview_A_surge_in_ schools.html.*

22. Meharg and Arnusch.

23. William Tordoff, *Government and Politics in Africa*, Fourth Ed., Bloomington, IN: Indiana University Press, 2002, pp. 168-195.

24. Yochuku Ofoka Yobolisa, "Nigeria: Pensions—Hanging Fate of Retired Military Personnel," allAfrica.com, December 23, 2009, available from allafrica.com/stories/200912240111.html?page=2.

25. *Ibid.*

26. Richard Dowden, *Africa: Altered States, Ordinary Miracles*, New York: Public Affairs, 2009, p. 53.

27. "Jane's World Armies: Botswana," *Jane's Information Group*, updated December 2, 2009, available by subscription only.

28. Dan Henk, "The Botswana Defence Force: Evolution of a Professional African Military," *African Security Review*, Vol. 13, No. 4, 2004, available from *www.iss.co.za/pubs/asr/13No4/EHenk.htm*;

29. *Ibid.*

30. Dan Henk, *The Botswana Defence Force in the Struggle for an African Environment*, New York: Palgrave MacMillan, 2007; U.S. Department of State Background Note: Botswana, updated December 2009, available from *www.state.gov/r/pa/ei/bgn/1830.htm*.

31. "Pirates Given 15 Year Jail Term In Somaliland Regional Court," Somaliland Government News Site, Hargiesa, Somaliland, February 17, 2010, available at *www.somalilandgov.com/*.

32. "Berbera College Business Plan," Hargeisa, Somaliland, available from *www.berberacollege.com/index.php?id=95&parent_id=86&lname=Business%20Plan*.

33. Niger Delta Development Commission Website, Skills Acquisition page, available from *nddc.gov.ng/?page=program&id=2*.

34. "Berbera College Business Plan."

35. Festus Owete, "Reps pass bill to promote Nigerian participation in oil industry," *Next News* (Nigerian and African News), October 23, 2009 available from *234next.com/csp/cms/sites/Next/Home/5473137-146/Reps_pass_bill_to_promote_Nigerian.csp.*

36. Caroline Duffield, "Will amnesty bring peace to Niger Delta?" *BBC News Africa*, October 5, 2009, available from *news.bbc.co.uk/2/hi/africa/8291336.stm.*

37. *Ibid.*

38. Augustine Ikelegbe, "The Economy of Conflict in the Oil Rich Niger Delta Region of Nigeria," *African and Asian Studies*, Vol.5, No. 1, 2006, p. 49.

39. Greg Mortenson and David Oliver Relin, *Three Cups of Tea: One Man's Mission to Promote Peace...One School at a Time*, New York: Penguin Books, 2006.

40. Robert Muggah, "Comparing DDR and Durable Solutions: Some Lessons from Ethiopia," *Humanitarian Exchange Magazine*, Issue 39, June 2008, available from *www.odihpn.org/report.asp?id=2913.*

41. Massimo Fusato, "Disarmament, Demobilization, and Reintegration of Ex-Combatants," *Beyond Intractability Knowledge Base Essay Series*, July 2003, available from *www.beyondintractability.org/essay/demobilization/.*

42. Ernest Harsch, "Reintegration of Ex-combatants: When War Ends; Transforming Africa's Fighters into Builders," Vol. 19, No. 3, October 2005, p. 1, available from *www.un.org/ecosocdev/geninfo/afrec/vol19no3/193combatant.html.*

43. See *www.mod.go.ke/?page_link=kma.*

44. "Historical Vignette 121: Corps Construction in Sub-Saharan Africa," U.S. Army Corps of Engineers Website, available from *www.usace.army.mil/History/hv/Pages/121-AfricaCivicAction.aspx.*

45. *Ibid.*

46. U.S. Army Corps of Engineers Commanding General Organizational Chart on U.S. Army Corps of Engineers Website, available from *www.usace.army.mil/about/HQORG/Pages/ CECGCommandingGeneral.aspx*.

47. *Ibid.*

48. *Ibid.*

49. "Academics" page, Annapolis, MD: U.S. Naval Academy, available from *www.usna.edu/academics.htm*; "Academics" Page, Boulder, CO: U.S. Air Force Academy, available from *www.usafa. af.mil/information/factsheets/factsheet.asp?id=9410*.

50. Samwel Kumba, "Bust-up with leaders a blessing for ex-KAF soldier," *Daily Nation*, January 22, 2010, available from *www.nation.co.ke/News/-/1056/847690/-/vpemu8/-/index.html*; "Kenya Armed Forces Technical College" page of the Kenyan Air Force Website, available from *www.mod.go.ke/Kafsite/Kaftec.htm*.

51. "Contemporary Army Operational Activities" page of the Kenyan Army Website, available from *www.mod.go.ke/Armysite/ currentoperations.htm*.

52. "Jane's Sentinel Security Assessment - Central Africa," *Armed Forces: Kenya*, November 10, 2009, available by subscription only.

53. "China Addresses Employment of Discharged Military Officers," *People's Daily Online* (news organ of the Central Committee), June 2009, in English, available from *english.peopledaily. com.cn/90001/90776/90785/6670274.html*; "The Great Global Officer Shortage," August 29, 2009, Strategy Page, online military affairs article aggregator, available from *www.strategypage.com/ htmw/htatrit/20090829.aspx*.

54. "China Addresses Employment of Discharged Military Officers," *People's Daily Online*, June 2009, in English, available from *english.peopledaily.com.cn/90001/90776/90785/6670274.html*.

55. Dr. Garth Shelton and The Wits University Peace Studies Group, "Case Study Demobilisation in Uganda," *Demobilisation and its Aftermath: A Profile of South Africa's Demobilised Military*

Personnel, Monograph No 59, Pretoria, South Africa: Institute for Security Studies (ISS) August 2001, available from *www.issafrica. org/Pubs/Monographs/No59/Chap3.html.*

56. *Ibid.*

57. "Military Training for Civilian Careers," *Occupational Outlook Quarterly,* Washington, DC: Bureau of Labor Statistics (BLS), 2007, available from *www.bls.gov/opub/ooq/2007/spring/art02.pdf.*

58. "Jane's World Armies: Botswana," *Jane's Information Group,* updated December 2, 2009, available by subscription only.

59. "Jane's Sentinel Security Assessment - Central Africa," *Armed Forces: Kenya,* July 14, 2009, available by subscription only.

60. Dr. Steven Metz, *Refining American Strategy in Africa,* Carlisle, PA: Strategic Studies Institute, U.S. Army War College, February 1, 2000, available from *www.strategicstudiesinstitute.army. mil/pubs/display.cfm?PubID=199.*

61. *Ibid.*

62. *Ibid.*

63. Dr. Donovan C. Chau, *U.S. Counterterrorism in Sub-Saharan Africa: Understanding Costs, Cultures, and Conflicts,* Carlisle, PA: Strategic Studies Institute, U.S. Army War College, August 27, 2008, available from *www.strategicstudiesinstitute.army.mil/pubs/ display.cfm?pubID=821.*

64. Phillip Van Neikerk, "Africa's Leadership Vacuum," *Current History,* May 2009, pp. 232-234, available from EBSO Host, *ejscontent.ebsco.com.ezproxy.mercyhurst.edu/ContentServer.aspx? target=http%3A%2F%2Fwww.currenthistory.com%2Fpdf_org_ files%2F108_718_232.pdf.*

www.ingramcontent.com/pod-product-compliance
Lightning Source LLC
Chambersburg PA
CBHW060006300526
45794CB00003B/1117